C000022274

Chasing

Unicorns

Roshan B. Karki

Roshan Karki

ISBN:0615475264
ISBN-13:978-0615475264

For Dr. James Pollock, Poet Roy Bentley
Sanjit Pradhananga, Rebecca Biancofiore and
Rajendra Thakurathi who motivated me to become a
better poet.

Chasing Unicorns

CONTENTS

	Acknowledgments	ii
1	A Trip for Eternity	4
2	Black and White Game	6
3	Blink of a Blue Light	7
4	Chasing Unicorns I	8
5	Child in One Second	9
6	Dance with the Unknown Lady	10
7	Deep in Heaven	11
8	Don't want to be the Honors Student anymore	12
9	Dreams	13
10	Drink with my Grandfather	14
11	Echoes of some Imaginations	15
12	First Kiss	16
13	Freedom	17
14	Gadfly's Zoo I	18
15	Gentlemen Spoke about our Generation	19
16	Green	20
17	Hissing Bamboo Sticks	21

18	I sold Cars and Bought Pigs	22
19	Imagine you are John Lennon	24
20	Lady with the Lamp	25
21	Life and Lie	26
22	Moving Upstairs	28
23	People in the Pub	29
24	Rain	30
25	Snake on a Horse	31
26	Summary of the Sea	32
27	The Farmer	33
28	The Moon	34
29	Thirty Two Suggestions for the Brain	35
30	Through the Unknown Doors	36
31	Verse of the Universe	37
32	Volcano	38
33	We know nothing like the Sky Does	39

Bonus poems   (40- 57)

1.   Bow of the Rainbow

2.   Death of a Fellow Politician

3.   Fear and Regret of a Lifetime

4. I like my Life

5. Lantern in a Lighthouse

6. Lord Randall's Library

7. Man and the Moth

8. Milky Way Galaxy

9. Moisture in the Woods

10. Monk made Blue Money

11. Philosophy of Death

12. October 16

13. The Art of Thinking

14. The Mystical Marriage

15. The Waterfall

16. Chasing Unicorns II

17. Chasing Unicorns III

    (From the perspective of a Loras College
    student)

18. Witch mother

    About the author

Roshan Karki

Chasing Unicorns

ACKNOWLEDGMENTS

Chasing Unicorns

A Trip for Eternity

A mother tells a story to her son. "Suddenly
the angel awakes and transfigures into the monster
who feasts on sailors and knights.
But the blind sailor lingers behind.
Sea, must you be unkind?"
She stops
as though the sea had suddenly frozen
The Sound of drowning comes from the shore

The next day, the villagers bring the sailor's body
from the sea
Like stars- his forehead is so cold
Like monsters- his mouth swallowing the stories
untold
The mother and the son tear like the sea

The boy asks, "Why did not your ring save him?"
The mother hands him an oar and says in a voice
As dead as his father
"Remember the story last night son. Kill the monster
And bring back my ring.
Do not change with seasons."

He is not sailing paper boats tearing his father's book
Anymore.
He is rowing a boat in a sea.
He pierces the sea with his oar like needles
He rows on colorless blood.
The sound of waves receding sound paler then his
Systole and diastole

The sea waves are his compass now
The aura on the hill reminds him of the angel.
Cruel sun reminds him of the dragon
Him of the dragon. Can sea be the monster?
He thinks and he thinks.
Then he grows a little older
Like the sea waves are floating
the dead bodies away.
He is not that much of a sailor now, he is a thinker
His hands have become his oars now; he is a boat
floating on waves
He is a monster floating on tears
Finally he is a prey floating on a boat

Will the sea swallow him tonight?
The sea is no water
The sea is a monster with angel's clothing and
ornaments on.
The sea seems to be attracting
Billions of other sons

Black and White Game

Dead horse looks courageous
Lying beside the two players
But it does not move on its own

Blink of a blue light

Blink of a blue light
attracts everyone's eye
In a corner next to pharmacy

Melisa dances in there
Swinging her body around the pole
Exposes her half breast out
To make a happier world

What will Melisa do next?
The crowd is loud and anxious
After Melisa repeats her original steps
The crowd fades

Melisa wakes up in the morning
Packs her briefcase
Her honors degree
She wears her white coat
And follows the sound of siren
To the area of red light.

Chasing Unicorns

My body was pierced with thousand invisible
arrows
Unable to catch any unicorns
I laid flat on the ground
The sun rays fell right through
Where I bled

Unicorns came and sniffed me like a bear
They neither moaned nor cried
Nor did they heal me
With their magical tears

The sound of a waterfall became clearer
Took my arrows out one by one
For the first time
I dared to find the difference
Between my imaginary battle field
And the green field

I stood up like a man
Looked at the horizon
I saw another hill there
Undiscovered
I saw a new hope there
My new life
My new Unicorns

Child in One Second

A Russian lady sat across from me on a train
Brown eyes and blue veins in her neck
Probably around her thirties

She looked at me and I looked at her
Our glances struck like a lightning bolt
Everything stopped for a while
The earth's rotation, people travelling
and our own breathing

My eyeballs receded toward the sockets
We were travelling through endless space
and time
Maybe we conceived a child
A beautiful one
In my mind

Dance with the Unknown lady

Couples usually dance together

So I was left alone
To escape the odd stares
I found a unknown lady
Lost like me

We started slow
A set of footsteps seeking unison
Then the night grew strange, as life can be

As the songs changed our dance changed
And sometimes I looked into her eyes
And sometimes she looked into mine

As the dawn approached
Wind burst open the curtains
Changing the dance floor
Lights became hallucinations
Melodies turned to howls

We grasped each other tight
Tying a knot
Memories changed forever

Deep in Heaven

The doors are flexible
And her cheeks are rosy
There are no lights there
He wants to pass through
So he lights one

A lamp that fills with oil
Once it burns
It smells
Nothing like fancy perfumes

Knock on the doors
Come slowly
Light up the lamps
Keep up the postures

And dwell
In the depths
The depths of heaven

Don't Want to be the Honors Student Anymore

It's been a week
Cell phone is dead

Don't look in the mirror
Don't think about life

Fish in the aquarium
Still healthy and alive
And wondering
This guy does not want to be
The honors student anymore

Dreams

Further you go, further it gets
Sometimes nothing is left
Except few foot prints and horse dungs
Dreams are like wild horses

May be climb a tree
When the spring comes, fruit ripens
The horses may come and graze around
Chances are you may jump on one of them

Never ride a horse fast
Never go for elephants either
Who knows that horse might knock you off
And you may find yourself
Among same horse dungs

Drink with my Grandfather

The grapes are fully ripe and almost rotten
Time for my grandfather to pluck them
Such grapes take less time to ferment
My grandfather was once a military man

Smoke ferments the grapes into wine

He calls me for a drink
Fascinates me he will be young again
Finally he convinces me
He is too young to be my grandfather

The bottle is half full now

Right grandfather
You are not my grandfather
God created me
God is my grandfather

The bottle is half empty now

You are right grandfather
You are not my grandfather
I came from the chimpanzees
Chimpanzee is my grandfather

The bottle is gone. It's morning
He is among the paddy fields
I whisper " Hey Grandfather.
Last night you were my real Grandfather."

Echoes of some imagination

Who am I?
Am I you?
If I created you
Then you should not be here breathing me

First Kiss

Your cheeks looked like apples
Your lips were wet
Did not want to touch your breasts
But
Could not hold on
And I kissed right on your lips
You were asleep
Call me a cat

Freedom

I took out the silk turbine off my head
Set it along the currents of northern breeze
On a roof of a train
I let it go from my hands
And declared its freedom

Gadfly's zoo I

Gadfly was my captain and a narcissist
when we were stationed at Vietnam. Once he did
not shoot his enemy
Because he looked just like him
After the war was over
Gadfly disappeared

Years passed and I was traveling along the
mountains in Tibet
Suddenly I saw a hill with colorful trees
Later I heard Gadfly had bought that hill and
Opened Gadfly's zoo
I went to meet Gadfly and Gadfly acted like God.
He fenced up the whole hill and permitted people
At his will
He offered me to pass rest of my life there
Taking care of them

People and everyone, welcome to Gadfly's zoo
Welcome and welcome.
Look at the tigers with deep blue eyes,
Moths like golden butterflies

People and everyone, welcome to Gadfly's zoo
Can you see the magicians flying in the sky?

Welcome to Gadfly's Zoo. Gadfly's zoo is home
of God.

Gentlemen spoke about our generation

Once gentlemen in leather shoes
Spoke to us about our generation
Beers and lesbians
Overconsumption and unpunctuality

Looked at him and gave him a smile
Came out and smoke a cigarette
All I wanted to say him was
Tomorrow we are going to lead this world

Green

Green is our eye
Green is the sky
Green in the emerald
Green is the caterpillar
Green is the poison
Green in the army
Green is our heart
Go Green

Hissing Bamboo Sticks

An old woman had planted a shrub of bamboos
Near my house when I was a kid
There a pair of doves had built their nests
The bamboos looked colorful during the days
But on the nights they hissed
Making strange but beautiful sound
Next morning the bamboos would get taller
After the old woman died
We cut those bamboos
To make her a carriage
For her to reach the paradise

I sold Cars and bought Pigs

I used to be almost happy when people
Used to curl in a line around my restaurant
The line looked like a pig's tail
I had a special ingredient.
I used pork for everything.
Pork in chicken salad, pork in vegetable salad
Pig's fat for butter

One day while I was driving I saw a big pig
snoring and chasing me
"Think about afterlife" it said
Thought for a while, decided to go to heaven
I opened a pig farm
Probably pigs do not know about family planning
Within three months they were everywhere
Pigs in the living room
Pigs in the guest room
Piglets watch Family Guy

Sean calls himself my best friend
He makes me smoke dried maple leaves saying
that is weed
Also he kicks my pigs wearing the new party
shoes I had gifted
On my birthday

Nena calls herself my girlfriend but threatens me.
She says " Darling! Let's run away from all this.
Do you have a car?" I say " No, I have pigs."
How can I run away with a girl I met just three
months ago ?

At my job interview I talk to person.
A big pile of resume is between us.
He asks, " Where do you see yourself in next five minutes? "
"What do you have for transportation?"
"Pigs will that work ?" I said
"I am sorry but you cannot have this job." He said
Thank you. Now I can watch my pigs for a whole day

I think of pigs then heaven
For me
Cars will give accidents, pigs will give salvation
I sold cars and bought pigs

Imagine you are John Lennon

Imagine you are John Lennon
Happy and high
And fly with that imagination
On the blue skies
Like a bird
Till someone shoots you down

Lady with the Lamp

She stood at the door
Between two rooms of my life and death
Holding a lamp in her hand
She dropped her tears
Like wax melting from a white candle

And she asked, "Hey Soldier, are you still there
?"
I said, "Yes Lady. I am still there
Next to you holding your hand
Standing between life and death."
Then she blew off her lamp and went away

Life and Lie

I conjured colorful paints on a blank and black
canvass and her cry harmonized the sound of
congested midnight train from heaven to hell
As years passed by she stopped believing the train is
toy
I took her out for a walk in circular track.

I took my daughter Mona Lisa past the black forest
down the hill, where the black and white butterflies
sucked insect blood, colorful moths hovered around
flowers
There black scarecrows made deep blue love,
Swastikas scared birds
And falling leaves showed us the path down the crest

And past the black villages
Pasted on oval grenades, where night vision
helicopters blocked the blue sky
shadows stabbed other shadows, and finally the
budget is allocated to dig graves
Orphan children came and showed us our way

We passed the marble coated court where
rusted statue of justice woke up from coma
and suicide. Lawyers read books of money and power
in frantic
tone for their funeral
And big falling hammer showed us our way

And she walked past her life
through sunny days and ebony nights

When I switched sunny days with ebony nights
Like raptor kites with tether kites

Her shadow walked past the gates of heaven
Where she still dreams
Is there any lie to show her path towards salvation?
There's a lie in Mona Lisa's smile
For I swapped truth with lies
For I am life

Moving Upstairs

Rebels may come anytime
So may thieves
Ram and his three month old son
Move their goats
From barn to balcony
A flash of torchlight eyes the infinity
Then they lock their main door
With a long breathe
They move upstairs

People in the Pub

People in thousands
Came to the pub
And always spoke to us politely
We stood like pillars
And took their orders
They never called us burger guys
They never said goodbye

Rain

Tears from the blue eye
Drops slowly
And it kisses the sea

Snake on a Horse

I get a recurring dream
A snake is on a head of a horse
The mare gallops steady in the direction
Snake shows her

The mare has no saddle
She does not have a name
But the snake sleeps on her crest
And drinks from her breast

The mare then goes to the green fields
It sniffs the grass
It finds a passage
Which leads to a hut

The snake crawls
And wakes me up
I ride the mare fast and furious

I look around in the town
When everyone is sleeping
I may be its foe
I may be its friend

But when I pass the green fields
I get a cold feeling
The snake may be sleeping
In my bed

Summary of the Sea

Dew droplets make up the sea
Similar should be the life force
Small events around the ocean make
Your Sun, Moon and the Universe

I pass my days looking at a blue waterfall
Dropping from heights
With an insurmountable current
And matching it with the
 sound of my heartbeat

Monsoon is coming
This time we will plant different breed
And wait for the harvest

Row safe on tides
Till then goodbye

The Farmer

The farmer wakes up early in the morning
Goes to his fields and waters the crops
He fertilizes them carefully
Looks at the sun
Thinks about the harvest

As the harvest nears the crops get yellowish
Unknown pestilence attacks them
The farmer tries to save them
The morning dew on the green leafs
Acts like acid and burns the plant
Finally they die and decay
The farmer then waits for another harvest

God must be a farmer

The Moon

Alice you are beautiful and charming
But you can be more
I ask you
Do you want to be the moon?

Alice you are bright
But you can be more
So I ask you
Do you want to be the moon?

You look lonely Alice
Still you can be more
And I ask you
Do you want to be the moon?

Thirty Two Suggestions for the Brain

Eat this, don't eat this
Eat cucumbers five times a day
Hear our   songs. Don't hear our songs

Go there. Do not go there.
Go there five times a day.

How do I know what to do and what not to
If there are thirty two suggestions in my brain?

Through the Unknown Doors

Once again
I am entering
Through the unknown doors
And trespassing in your territory

Lights pale and yellow fall on the playground
Years have past
You do not even call me for a drink

You shout at me like a criminal
And I run away barefoot
Get lost in your playground

May be if you were my mother
You would love me
You are scary, addictive and parasitic
Still I like you

I am in so love with you
But you make me feel
So lonely
So bare

Verse of the Universe

He begs and begs and that makes him
 a millionaire

He gives sons after sons and that makes him a god

He looks after you till you have your son and that
Makes him a father

He prays and prays and that makes him a priest

He tries to win you by force and that makes him
A loser

Life is a universe of possibilities

Volcano

Ashes on the mountain
Rises up to heaven
The lava
Flows from the mountain's face
Towards the village
The birds watch the volcano erupting
Without fear

We know nothing like the Sky does

The sky makes thunder anytime it wants
The sky makes rain anytime it wants
It can hide anything
It can hide heaven
It can hide the whole universe
We know nothing like the sky does

Bonus poems

1. Bow of the Rainbow

A big arrow ready to leave its spectral bow
Caught the sight of my eye
When I was a child
Nailed to strange passengers
With beautiful women
And luxurious cuisine
And it aimed its way towards heaven.

2. Death of a Fellow Politician

One night Mr. Big woke up and found
Sleeping pills did not give him any sleep
He stood up numb recalling his days
He did not think about skeletons
People reported seeing as ghosts
During the civil war while he was a senator

He did not think about all the money he corrupted
Instead memories of children came
Raindrops and spring birds
His years in college

Then came the sound of humming bird
He smiled and started giggling
He took a long breathe and died with a smile
A smile on his face

3. Fear and Regret of a Lifetime

You should have seen me
Ten years before, when I was ten
Eyes with a golden spark
I would have lighten the world

You should have seen me
Twenty years before, when I was twenty
I was a rebellious fire
I would have burnt the world

You should have seen me
Forty years before when I was forty
I was a father
I would have saved the world

You should see me now
Eighty years old, ready to die
Eyes full of tears
For have done nothing in life

4. I like my Life

The news breaks my family fuzz
Of tanks roaring and glass cracking
It scares my daughter's heart
Young kid sensible to life

I am middle classed man, I work hard everyday
Take care of the pile of files
Still some bills may be left unfulfilled
But the voices seldom roar at night
Somehow it has always passed

We picnic among the trees
We walk with the breeze
We have everything we need

But once again
I am lost between the crowd
The memories of my daughter are in his head
Despite the cracks
I like how I am living my life

5. Lantern in a Lighthouse
(Inspired by the movie " Inception")

Reek sees himself in a faint lighthouse
In his dreams
Where he is carrying a lantern
Looking through a broken window
Searching for the stars

It's been so long any shimmering ships with
Polished decks have not appeared on the horizon
Long before the ships marched with
Their windy sails on

Reek then lights the lighthouse with the lantern
The bricks burn and fall off one by one
On the dark brown ocean
Creating concentric ripples
Which dissolves into the deepest core of Reek's
heart
Creating distorted visions
Taking Reek into deeper nightmares

The waves rise upon the lighthouse
Like Reek used to dance a long time ago
The lighthouse then collapses into the Ocean
A thin air blows off the lantern
Reek wakes up back in reality

6. Lord Randall's Library

The children march to his schools
They pay their bills
Lord Randall tames them
Bulky books
Vague visions
Slim sticks
Discipline

Tomorrow they will graduate
Lord Randall will be still young
When their children will go to school
Lord Randall will be still young
And it makes me wonder on few things if
Lord Randall is wrong

7. Man and the Moth

A child is born he learns to fly
Ambition takes him high and high
Slowly he starts to get old
The doors will start to close
Finally he flies through the door
Just like a moth

8. Milky Way Galaxy

The world is a balloon
Missiles have punctured it all along
It's funny
We are whirling around the milky way Galaxy

People die and people cry
We are whirling into the Milky Way Galaxy
It makes me wonder
If you want to go back to the forest
To our origin

9. Moisture in the woods

Here comes the night with the wind
The rain in falling on the coconut trees
Tomorrow the day will be moist
There will be moisture in the woods

The flood may come and wash us all
May be we will escape on our rafts
But there will be rain and there will be woods
There will be moisture in the woods.

10. Monk made blue money

From the Himalayas he came
Looked at the city
With a gentle breathe
Soon he forgot he is a monk

Money for him was blue in color
Luck found him a beautiful lady
He opened casinos, restaurants and bars
Where people came and sang cheerfully

He made millions
and donated them all
Then he went back
Back to the Himalayas

11. Philosophy of Death

Plan in your notebook ahead
What would you do if you were dead?

May be you would be a mummy
In a museum's cage
May be ride a rocket
Into the space

May be go to a heaven or a hell
If heaven; pack a bell
If hell
Half boiled eggs

Travelers plan for their vacation ahead
If life is a journey, death should be a vacation

12. October 16

I looked outside,
The leaves from the trees were falling
It was October
Summer had passed away and winter was   coming

Inside candles were burning
A breeze of wind came
The room went dark

My mother took out a calendar
Marked October 16th with a coal tar
"Good things did not happen in the history this
  day." she said

China tested its first atomic missile
The sixth coalition attacked Napoleon Bonaparte
Queen Marie Antoinette was beheaded.

I grabbed the calendar and tore it
Made paper boats and sailed in a nearby stream
Few years later I walked past that stream
I became a robber. Robbed houses for ornaments
and diamond rings
One day someone robbed me
I returned back home

The stream had turned red
On my reflection wrinkles had started growing
On face and forehead

I saw the torn calendar on the wall

October 16th was marked
An old woman was near by
I asked, " Why October sixteenth is marked ?"
She said, " That's your birthday."

13. The Art of Thinking

You are the slave
It's your master
It will keep on slaving you
Till you control your thoughts down
Thinking is like controlling mad horse

14. The Mystical Marriage

Ying and yang
Shake and tremble
They fertilize and fuse
To form eggs
Inside our bodies
Takes place
Small 'big bangs'
The mystical marriage

15. The Waterfall

To and fro
A waterfall
A lady swings
On a rope
Then she jumps
With a suspended motion
Into a lake

She
Shows
A diamond sword
Thus tempting the men
Tempted by her beauty
They
Jump into the lake
They turn into
Sea horses

16. Chasing Unicorns II

Once white unicorns
In my golden dreams
Showed me a staircase
Paved with silver
They tempted me

The thick fur of unicorns are
Like the wildest sea waves
But they hide and seek
Making the spiral slippery

When my eyes fall below
People whisper in low tones
The first ladder was made of stones
Government and Gods
Once walked up the stairs
Covering it up with silver

I refuse, I resist
That's your ladder, that's not mine
I will travel, I might run
I will find my unicorns

17.Chasing Unicorns III

(From the perspective of Loras College student)

Blue eyes and beers
Career and coolers
Dreams and destiny
I am walking and chasing my unicorns

Bulls and bulldozer
Death and drugs
Piracy and conspiracy about
Government and Gods
Look
I have done nothing wrong
I was just walking
And chasing my Unicorns

18. Witch mother

I wonder what sin had the boy done
Not to have his own mother
He calls an unknown woman " mother,
mother."

She won't drop her affection
On the boy
A witch is inside her
She is her stepmother
She acts a witch mother

About the author

Roshan Karki is from a hilly region in Dolakha, Nepal. Since his early years he showed an interest in fiction and poetry and seldom wrote for enjoyment. He began writing passionately after attending Loras College in Dubuque, Iowa, USA.

"Chasing Unicorns,"Karki's first book, is a collection of poems written during his two years at Loras College. The poems reflect his experiences at Loras College and emotional transition from teenager to the early phase of adulthood.

CPSIA information can be obtained at www.ICGtesting.com
Printed in the USA
BVOW07s1053060813

327953BV00001B/9/P